I0842136

Mini Lessons in Story Starting

Three quick lessons for fiction writers.

By Janie Sullivan

Other books by Janie Sullivan

Non-Fiction

Janie's Memoir Writing Class:
A Memoir Guide/Workbook for Those Who Have
Reached a "Certain Age"

Do You Call Yourself a Writer?

Develop and Deliver an Online Course

A Tuscan Dining Experience

Creating Characters That Speak:
Using Character Sketches and Dialogue Effectively

Writing from A to Z:
A Blog Series from The Center for Writing
Excellence

Why Do My Characters Behave That Way?
Three Aspects of Character Development

Family Anthology:
How to Turn Your Family Files into a Book the
Whole Family Can Enjoy

A System of Five:
Five Practices that Guarantee Excellent Faculty

Anthologies

Picking Dandelions
The Johnston Family Anthology

First, Second, and Third Annual Fiction Anthologies
(Center for Writing Excellence Fiction Anthologies)

Fiction

The Wise Acres Cozy Mystery Series

Book One: *The Mahjong Murder Club*

Book Two: *Fortune or Folly??* (Due out Spring, 2018)

Co-Authored Fiction
with Rhonda Jackson

Alexis' Aggravation:
Murder in the Southwest

One Hundred Years From London
Volume of Short Stories for Light Reading

All books can be found at Janie Sullivan's Author Page on Amazon.com: http://www.amazon.com/-/e/B008S027GO

Mini Lessons in Story Starting

Three Quick Lessons for Fiction Writers

Mini Lessons in Story Starting

All rights reserved.

Copyright © 2018 by Janie Sullivan

All rights reserved. No part of this book may be used or reproduced by any means, graphic, electronic, or mechanical, including photocopying, recording, taping or by any information storage retrieval system without the written permission of the publisher except in the case of brief quotations embodied in critical articles and reviews. This is a work of fiction. All of the characters, names, incidents, organizations, and dialogue in this novel are either the products of the authors' imaginations or are used fictitiously.

For information:
The Center for Writing Excellence, a Small Press
480 Bray Central Drive, #11204
Allen, Texas 75013

Janie's Email: janiewrites1@gmail.com

ISBN-13: 978-1985283756

ISBN-10: 1985283751

Published by: The Center for Writing Excellence, a
Small Press
Printed in the United States of America
Date:

Table of Contents

Mini Lessons in Story Starting

In this three-lesson booklet, you will generate story ideas that you can use later, and you will learn techniques for getting new story ideas whenever you need them.

Lesson 1: Characters

Story Elements

There are many kinds of writing, but if nothing happens in the piece of writing, it is a description, an article, or perhaps a philosophical discourse, but not a story.

There are three elements a story needs:

- Something must happen. It happens to someone or someone does something.
  - Element One: A character
- The thing that happens; happens somewhere.
  - Element Two: A setting

- The problem that makes something happen.
  - o Element Three: A conflict

Story Ideas

There are many ways to come up with story ideas, but the following exercises will give you not only the idea, but it will help you with the conflict, character, and setting.

Try starting with one of the elements listed above. You can choose any of the elements but use it to determine the other two elements. Here are some examples to get you started:

Using *Conflict* as your first element, the character(s) and setting will follow naturally. For example, if your conflict is bullying, answer these questions:

1. Who is the bully? (character)
   a. What motivates him or her?
2. Who are the victims? (character)
   a. How do they respond?
3. What kind of school do the characters attend? (setting)
   a. Where is the school located?
   b. Public school? Private school?

Or try using *Setting* as the first element. Example: A Mississippi cotton plantation just before the Civil War. Use the setting to determine the conflict, then the character:

1. Slaves forcibly separated from their children. (Conflict)
2. Pregnant slave willing to risk her life to keep her unborn child. (Character)

Or you could start with a *Character* trait. Try this one: A woman (or man) who is obsessed with neatness.

1. Conflict idea:
    a. In what situation would the character's obsession with neatness become a problem?
    b. In what situation would she/he face a mess she/he couldn't control?
2. Setting idea:
    a. The character's ultra-organized apartment with its elaborate systems of cabinets, compartments, and labeled containers.

Character Ideas

How do you get ideas for characters? Here are five different ways. Think about how and when you can try any of these methods.

Method 1: People-watch.

Observe people who pass you on the street; go to a mall or a café and watch the people around you. Look at how they dress and present themselves, their facial expressions, their gestures, how they move, how they interact with each other. Try to imagine their lives. Be sure to jot down some notes before you forget – but be careful. You don't want to be accused of stalking someone!

Watch people in line at the supermarket – listen to their conversations, pay attention to what they're buying. Do they live by themselves or with children? Do they have pets? Do they cook a lot, or do they keep precooked food in their freezers? Are they planning a party? Or, are they drinking too much alone?

Every one of these people can become a fictional character in your stories. Make up interesting things about them.

Method 2: Get ideas from the newspaper.

Newspapers are a rich source of character ideas.

When you read about ordinary people in extraordinary situations, try to imagine the people behind the headlines. What might have caused a particular woman to shoot her husband? What kind of person might she be, and what might her husband have been like?

The people you imagine are likely to be very different from the real people involved in the news item. That's fine. They're fictional characters that you have invented. Now you can use them however you like in your stories.

Wedding announcements and obituaries are another great place to look for character ideas. Use your imagination to fill in the blank space around the information the newspaper reports.

Method 3: Get ideas from names.

A name triggers a complex set of associations, based on its sound and the way it looks on a page, based also on the people we have known or heard of with that name or similar names.

Take the names of famous people in the news and change them a bit to "protect the innocent" and work them into the story. For example, my writing partner and I named one of our characters Sara Pallon. She is a political figure in the story, although not running for Vice President, and in the end of the story she … but that would be giving it away. You will just have to read the book.

Here is an excerpt from the working copy of our novel. See how we worked the name into the story?

"Gimme a sec. I will look the number up in the reverse directory." McRae clicked the laptop keyboard a couple times. "Here it is: Sara Pallon. Say, isn't she the one who was running for VP a couple years ago?"

"No, that one spelled her name differently. This one is on the City Council. Wonder why the dead doc was calling her?"

Naming your characters with similar names as people in your life or on the news that you don't like and then killing them off in your story is much better than actually committing the crime!

Just names themselves, without being familiar to you, are wonderful sources for character development.

Take a moment to picture a woman named Hazel, a woman named Linda, a woman named Monique. What images do these names bring to mind?

The name Hazel makes me think of a plump seventy-year-old woman with graying hair in a bun. She wears no makeup and has deep lines along the sides of her mouth. She is wearing an apron and is baking cookies.

Your Hazel is probably completely different from mine. What does your Linda or Monique look like?

You can find names online. I recently needed a name for a character in a novel that was an actor who played a detective in the movies, but in the story was helping out the local sheriff and was using his "actor-who-plays-a-detective" status to "legitimize" his involvement with the sheriff.

I Googled "famous male actors' names" and then picked a first name (Ian) and a last name (Keaton) for my character's name.

Method 4: Mix and match.

Often, writers base characters on real people they know. That sometimes works well, but in other cases, it can be limiting. It can be hard to stop thinking of the real person and imagine the character separately.

Here's a different method to try: create a character that mixes aspects of several people you know.

For example, you might invent a character that is partly based on your father, partly based on one of your high school teachers, and partly based on your boss at work. Or, you might base a character on your father, but make that character a woman. You could base the character's physical appearance on a waitress you saw at a restaurant.

The result of each combination will be a character that shares similarities with all of these people but, at the same time, is different from all of them: unique. This might also keep you out of trouble with your friends and family.

They might suspect you modeled the character on them, but if enough of the traits are from other people, you can always proclaim your innocence.

Method 5: Turn characters into more characters.

Each character you create can be the seed of more character ideas.

Who is in your character's family? What are your character's parents like? Who is your character's best friend? Who is your character's enemy? What kind of person gets on your character's nerves? What kind of person attracts your character romantically or feels attracted by your character?

Brainstorm on questions like these, and then develop the answers into new characters.

Character Development

Once you have an idea for a character, you can start developing the character by imagining more aspects of this person and his or her life.

Here's a questionnaire that you can use to create character profiles and start developing the back story. Feel free to change any of the questions or add new ones:

1. What's the character's occupation?
2. What's the character's family like?

3. Is the character in a relationship? What's his or her partner like?

4. What is the character's home like? His or her neighborhood?

5. Does your character have hobbies? What does he or she enjoy doing?

6. What are your character's greatest strengths?

7. What are his or her greatest weaknesses?

8. What is his/her deepest desire?

9. What is his/her greatest fear?

10. What is something this character desperately wants to change about himself or herself?

11. What is something this character doesn't know about himself or herself?

Most of this information will not actually go into your stories, but it will help you to flesh out the characters in your own mind so that you can write about them in a convincing way.

Your answers to these questions can also become an endless source of story ideas.

Lesson 2: Conflict

So far, we have talked about five different techniques for generating character ideas. These are techniques you can use repeatedly to create new characters whenever you need them.

In this lesson, we'll look at how you can turn fictional characters into story ideas. To do this, you need to come up with ideas for story conflicts.

What is Conflict?

A story conflict is a problem facing the main character. This problem might be a romantic rival or a horde of attacking zombies. It might be an internal struggle; for example, the character has to overcome a particular fear or a bad habit. It could be related to current events; for example, the character is faced with a choice when budget cuts force a lay-off. Use what you have in front of you on the news, in the paper, on Facebook, etc.

Here are some examples of story conflicts:

- Mary falls in love with the perfect man, but she's already married to someone else.

- John wants to be president of his high school class, but he is terrified of public speaking.
- Twila has recurring dreams about a terrible crime.

Conflict is important because it makes things happen. If everything in your character's life is perfect, there is no reason for her to take action. There is no reason for anything to change. And no change equals no story.

Elements of Conflict

If readers care about the result of your story conflict, they will keep reading to find out what happens.

What makes readers care?

1. The result of the conflict matters a lot to your character.
2. The readers identify with your character – in other words, readers imagine themselves in your character's place.

Point of View

A first-person point-of-view character is a character whose perspective is used to tell the story. Readers see the story through that character's eyes, experiencing what that character experiences. You need to choose point of view when you identify the main characters. Who is telling the story?

Readers tend to identify with the viewpoint character and feel as if they're resolving the story's conflict along with him or her. They're frustrated when the character encounters obstacles and relieved when the obstacles are overcome. They're triumphant or in despair at the end of the story when the character either succeeds or fails.

When writing a short story, it's generally best to have one viewpoint character and develop a conflict that matters to that character. This gives your reader, who identifies with the character, a stake in what happens.

If the starting point for your story idea is the conflict instead of the character, then come up with a viewpoint character who will be directly affected by the result of that conflict.

Characters and Conflict

Here are seven ways to turn a character idea into an idea for conflict, which gives you the seed for a story.

You can repeat the techniques with new characters and come out with a completely different story every time!

1. Imagine a situation in which your character has the chance to obtain his or her deepest desire... but there is a terrible obstacle in the way. (What obstacle? You decide.)
2. Imagine a situation that forces your character to face his or her greatest fear in order to achieve an important goal.
3. Imagine a situation that forces your character into a major struggle with someone he or she hates.
4. Imagine a situation that threatens to cut your character off from a person he or she loves. How does your character react?
5. Imagine a situation in which your character must overcome his or her greatest weakness or risk losing something he or she cares about deeply.

6. Imagine a situation in which something your
   character doesn't know about himself or herself
   is about to ruin his or her life, unless the
   character is capable of making drastic changes.
7. Imagine a situation in which your character
   must choose between two of the people he or
   she cares for the most.

Can you think of other situations that would force
your character(s) to engage in conflict of some
kind?

What is Plot?

The word *plot* is used to describe the structure of a
story's action: the main events of the story and the
order in which they happen.

1. The five elements of plot are:
   a. The character and the conflict are introduced.
      (***Exposition***)
   b. The character struggles with the
      conflict. (***Rising Action***)
   c. The character's struggle builds to a win-or-
      lose moment that will determine if the story
      ends happily or not. (Story Climax)
   d. Action/struggle decreases. (Falling Action)

e. The character either is either successful or unsuccessful in resolving the conflict. (*Resolution*)

If you have a character idea and a conflict idea, you have everything necessary to plot your story.

Lesson 3: Setting

In Lessons 1 and 2, we looked at lots of ways to come up with ideas for characters and story conflicts. In this final lesson, we're going to generate ideas for story settings.

Setting is Important

A story's *Setting* is the time and place of the story.

Examples of settings:

- A middle-class Phoenix suburb (present-day)
- The Shenandoah Valley during the Civil War
- London in 1849 – Filthy, cholera epidemic, etc.

The details of your story's setting create a world where your character can move around and the conflict can unfold.

Everything your character sees and touches depends on the setting. Your character's house, the clothes she wears, the secret shortcut she takes through the woods, the rain sprinkling down on her – all of this depends on the story's setting

Ideas for Setting

How do you choose a story's setting?

You can choose the setting because it's familiar to you, or because it's interesting, or because it adds something specific to your story's conflict.

You can also use your characters to get setting ideas. Here are some questions to help.

Character Setting Questionnaire:

1. What kind of home and neighborhood did you imagine for your character?
2. What are some of the items in your character's refrigerator? What's on your character's bookshelves? Is there anything under your character's bed? What's in your character's night table drawers?

3. Where has your character lived in the past?
   What kind of environment do you think
   your character grew up in?
4. What are your character's cultural roots?
5. What kind of schools did your character
   attend?
6. Did your character ever go to summer
   camp?
7. What is your character's workplace like?
8. If your character is married, did he or she
   go on a honeymoon, and where?
9. If your character is married, where do his
   or her in-laws live? What is their home like?
10. Where does your character go to relax?
    Where does your character go when he or
    she feels lonely?
11. Does your character have a secret place or a
    place where s/he goes to escape from
    her/his problems?
12. What's a place where your character feels
    extremely uncomfortable? A place where
    your character behaves badly?
13. What's a place your character has always
    wanted to visit? Would this place meet
    your character's expectations?

The answers to many of these questions can provide ideas for new story conflicts! A setting idea can become a story idea when it creates a problem of some kind for your character.

You can even leave "booby traps" in your setting and see if they turn into new story ideas. For example, if you set your story about a camping trip in a swamp where alligators live, maybe one of those alligators will creep up to your character's tent and create a story conflict. Or if you set your story in a hunting lodge with a cabinet full of guns in the bar, maybe someone will produce a story conflict by getting drunk and then picking up a gun.

Describing the Setting

You can make your setting come alive for the reader by including details that capture its special flavor. What sights, sounds, smells, sensations are typical of your setting or unique to it?

Here is an example of a description of Victorian London:

"London was foul, noisy and stinking. Its narrow streets squelched with mud and dung…. Ladies delicately lifted their skirts to cross the road and gave a coin to the ragged boys employed as crossing-sweepers, who brushed away just some of the dung and dust." (Victorian Interiors and More,

http://victoriandecorating.blogspot.com/2007/02/life-in-london-1849.html)

You don't have to list all these details together in a block of "description." Weave setting details throughout your story, using them where they fit naturally without interrupting the story's flow. How would you weave the information above in to a Show Me, don't Tell Me narrative in a story?

How to find details for your setting:

Observation. If your setting is somewhere you know well or someplace you can visit, record details in your Idea Journal so that you use them later.

- Books and articles about that time/place.
- Interviews with people from that time/place - either interviews you do yourself, or published interviews.
- Published journals and letters by people from that time/place. Related biographies.

- Magazines and newspapers from that time/place.
- Photos, movies, documentaries.

Bonus: Four Ideas to Get You Started in Four Genres

1. **YA Fiction**: Your character, a 14-year old boy, is reading his favorite book on the beach when he notices a boat slowly drifting to shore. It eventually lands near the teenager. A person, draped in pirate clothes, yells from the boat, "I have a treasure map and I need help. Are you in?"

2. **Fantasy Fiction**: In a realm where an advanced species of orcs hunt humans for sport, one person has found a way to turn the tide. Will his people, who struggle to survive in the brutal wilderness bordering the Orcish Kingdom, have it in them to rise up against their oppressors?

3. **Crime Fiction**: A large diamond disappears from the vault of a jewelry store. The owner of the store personally put it in the vault and set the timer on the lock. Three witnesses, an

employee and two customers, saw him go into the vault with the diamond. The next morning it is gone. There was no way to open the vault that night, even for the owner.

4. **Science Fiction**: Two children, a boy and a girl, decide to make a time capsule and bury it at the edge of a farm, under a big oak tree. While digging, they unearth a metallic object the size of a shoebox. It's shaped like a bullet and has the number 8 engraved on it. It appears to be a container, since it rattles when they shake it. However, there is no obvious way to open it.

About the author

Janie Sullivan, MBA, MAEd, has been teaching adult learners for over 25 years. She has taught online over 20 years, specializing in writing, communications, and small business applications. She was a faculty trainer for over 15 years at both the University and Community College levels. She has been published in several newspapers, magazines and online sites. She has a strong entrepreneurial background, having run a very successful project management documentation production company during the 90s.

Education
Masters of Business Administration
Masters of Education Administration
Bachelor of Arts in Journalism

Publications and Courses Written
21-courses comprising Online Teaching Strategies Certification
Novel: Alexis' Aggravation: Murder in the Southwest
Cozy Mystery Series: Wise Acres Cozy Mysteries, Book One: Mahjong Mystery Club. Book Two: Fortune or Folly?? (Due out in Spring 2018)

Anthology: One Hundred Years from London, Short Stories for Light Reading

Articles in Various Publishing Venues		
Newspapers	Websites	Magazines
The Missoulian

The Phillipsburg Mail

The Mesa Tribune

The Business Journal | eHow

Infobarrel

Demand Studios

Examiner.com

Suite 101

HubPages | Small Business Start-Up Magazine

The Adjunct Advocate |

www.ingramcontent.com/pod-product-compliance
Lightning Source LLC
Chambersburg PA
CBHW051927250726
48659CB00002B/889